VOODOO SHOP

Ruth Padel

Chatto & Windus
LONDON

Published by Chatto & Windus 2002

2 4 6 8 10 9 7 5 3 1

Copyright © Ruth Padel, 2002

Basil Bunting's 'The Spoils' from his *Complete Poems* is quoted by permission
of Bloodaxe Books. Sean O'Faolain's 'Lovers of the Lake' is quoted by
permission of Constable and Robinson Publishing Ltd.

First published in Great Britain in 2002 by
Chatto & Windus
Random House, 20 Vauxhall Bridge Road,
London SW1V 2SA

Random House Australia (Pty) Limited
20 Alfred Street, Milsons Point, Sydney,
New South Wales 2061, Australia

Random House New Zealand Limited
18 Poland Road, Glenfield,
Auckland 10, New Zealand

Random House South Africa (Pty) Limited
Endulini, 5A Jubilee Road, Parktown 2193, South Africa

Random House UK Limited Reg. No. 954009

A CIP catalogue record for this book
is available from the British Library

ISBN 0 7011 7301 7

Papers used by Random House are natural,
recyclable products made from wood grown in sustainable forests.
The manufacturing processes conform to the environmental
regulations of the country of origin.

Typeset by Deltatype Ltd, Birkenhead, Merseyside
Printed and bound in Great Britain by
Mackays of Chatham PLC

In memory of my father

with love

ACKNOWLEDGEMENTS

Many thanks to the editors of *After Pushkin*, ed. Elaine Feinstein (Carcanet, 1999), *Boomerang*, *The Dublin Review*, *The Erotic Review*, *The Feminist Review*, *The Forward Book of Poetry 2000*, *The Guardian*, *Journal of Literature and Aesthetics* (Kerala, South India), *London Magazine*, *London Review of Books*, *Last Words*, ed. Don Paterson and Jo Shapcott (Picador, 1999), *Everybody's Mother*, ed. L. Coggin and C. Marlow (Peterloo Poets, 2001), *Mslexia*, *New Writing 9*, ed. John Fowles and A. L. Kennedy (Vintage, 2000), *Poetry Ireland*, *Poetry London*, *Poetry Nation Review*, *Poetry Review*, *Private Eye*, *The Red Wheelbarrow*, *Rialto*, *Seshat*, *Stand*, *Times Literary Supplement*.

'Rattlesnakes and Rubies' was commissioned by BBC Radio 3's 'Word of Mouth' and shortlisted for the Forward Prize Best Individual Poem 2000. 'The Light that Casts a Shadow' was commissioned by Pier Productions for BBC Radio 4. 'Joinery' was commissioned for BBC Radio 3's 'Poetry Proms 2000'. 'Ruins of Holy Island on Lough Derg' was commissioned by the Ulster Museum (to accompany their watercolour, with the same title, by Bartholomew Watkins) and appeared in *A Conversation Piece*, ed. Adrian Rice and Angela Reid (Abbey Press & Ulster Museum Publications, 2002). 'Hey Sugar, Take a Walk on the Wild Side' was commissioned for the window of a delicatessen in the Salisbury Poetry Festival and first published on a tea-towel.

Many warm thanks to Elaine, Jo, John and Neil, who read and criticised; and my editors, Rebecca Carter and Christopher Reid.

CONTENTS

When Tigris floods snakes swarm in the city,
coral, jade, jet, between jet and jade, yellow . . .

Basil Bunting, 'The Spoils'

WRITING TO ONEGIN

(After Pushkin)

Look at the bare wood hand-waxed floor and long
White dressing-gown, the good child's writing-desk
   And passionate cold feet
Summoning music of the night, timbrels, gongs
And gamelans. And one neat pen, one candle
   Puckering its life out hour by hour. Is 'Tell
Him I love him' never a good idea? You can't
Wish this unlived – this world on fire, on storm
   Alert, till a shepherd's song
Outside, some hyperactive yellowhammer, bulbul,
Wren, amplified in hills and woods, tells her to bestow
   A spot of notice on the dawn.

'I'm writing to you. Well, that's it, that's everything.
You'll laugh, but you'll pity me too. I'm ashamed of this.
   I meant to keep it quiet. You'd never have known, if –
I wish – I could have seen you once a week. To mull over, day
And night, the things you say. Or what we say together.
   But word is, you're misogynist. Laddish. A philanderer
Who says what he doesn't mean (that's not how you come across
To me), who couldn't give a toss for domestic peace –
   Only for celebrity and showing off –
And won't hang round in a provincial zone
Like this. We don't glitter. Though we do,
   Warmly, truly, welcome you.

'Why did you come? I'd never have set
Eyes on a star like you, nor blundered up against
   This crazed not-sleeping, hour after hour
In the dark. I might have got the better of
My clumsy fury with constraint, my fret

For things I lack all lexica and phrase-book art
To get straight in my head. I might have been a faithful wife,
A mother. But that's all done with. This is Fate.
    God. Sorted. Here I am – yours, to the last breath.
I couldn't give my heart to anyone else.
My life till now has been a theorem, to demonstrate
    How right it is to love you. This love is love to death.

'I knew you anyway. I loved you, I'm afraid,
In my sleep. Your eyes, that denim-lapis, grey-sea
    Grey-green blue, that Chinese fold of skin
At the inner corner, that shot look
Bleeping "vulnerable" under the screensaver charm,
    Kept me alive. Every cell, every last gold atom
Of your body, was engraved in me
Already. Don't tell me that was dream! When you came in
    Staring round in your stripy brocade
Jacket, I nearly fainted. I was flame. I recognized
The you I'd always listened to – alone, when I wrote,
    Or tried to wrestle my scatty soul into calm.

'Wasn't it you who slipped through the transparent
Darkness to my bed and whispered love? Aren't you
    My guardian angel? Or is this arrant
Seeming: hallucination, thrown up by
That fly engineering a novel does, so
    Beguilingly, or poems? Is this mad?
Are there ways of dreaming I don't know?
Too bad. My soul has made its home
    In you. I'm here and bare before you: shy,
In tears. But if I didn't heft my whole self up and hold it there –
A crack-free mirror – loving you, or if I couldn't share it,
    Set it out in words, I'd die.

'I'll wait to hear from you. I must. Please let me hope.
Give me one look, from eyes I hardly dare
   To look back at. Or scupper my dream
By scolding me. I've given you rope
To hang me: tell me I'm mistaken. You're so much in
   The world; while I just live here, busy with harvest, songs
And books. That's not complaint. We live such different lives.
So . . . this is the end. It's taken all night.
   I'm scared to read it back; I'm faint
With shame and fear. But this is what I am. My crumpled bed,
My words, my open self. All I can do is trust
   The whole damn lot of it to you.'

She sighs. The paper trembles as she presses down
The pink wax seal. Outside, a milk mist clears
   From the shimmering valley. If I were her guardian
Angel, I'd divide myself. One half would holler
Don't! Stay on an even keel! Don't dollop over
   All you are, to a man who'll go to town
On his next little fling. If he's entranced today
By the way you finger your throat inside its collar,
   Tomorrow there'll be Olga, Nicole, Jane. But then I'd whisper
Go for it, petal. Nothing's as real as what you write.
His funeral, if he's not up to it. What we feel
   Is mortal, and won't come again.

So cut, weeks later, to an outside shot: the same girl
Taking cover ('Dear God, he's here, he's come!')
   Under fat red gooseberries, glimmering hairy stars:
The old, rude bushes she has hide-and-seeked in all
Her life, where mother tells the serfs to sing
   While picking, so they can't hurl
The odd gog into their mouths. No one could spy
Her here, not even the sun in its burn-time. Her cheeks

3

Are simmering fire.
We're talking iridescence, a Red Admiral's last tremble
Before the avid schoolboy plunks his net.
      Or imagine a leveret

Like the hare you shot, remember, at the country house,
Which ran round screaming like a baby?
      Only mine is shivering in papery winter corn,
While the hunter (as it might be, you) stomps his Hush
Puppies through dead brush. Everything's quiet.
      She's waited – how long? – ages: stoking pebbly embers
Under the evening samovar, filling
The Chinese teapot, sending coils of Lapsang Souchong
      Floating to the ceiling in the shadows, tracing O and E
In the window's black reflection, one finger
Tendrilling her own breath on the glass.
      Like putting a shell to your ear to hear the sea

When it's really your own red little sparkle, the echo
Of marching blood. She's asking a phantom world
      Of pearled-up mist for proof
That her man exists: that gamelans and timbrels
Won't evade her. But now, among
      The kitchen garden's rose-haws, mallow, Pernod-
Coloured pears, she unhooks herself thorn by thorn
For the exit aria. For fade-out. Suddenly there he is
      In the avenue, the man she's written to – Charon
Gazing at her with blazing eyes! Darth Vader
From *Star Wars*. She's trapped, in a house she didn't realize
      Was burning. Her letter was a gate to the inferno.

HEY SUGAR, TAKE A WALK ON THE WILD SIDE

Imagine we're two bottles of Strozzapieto
Di Padrone Olive Oil, the pond-green
    Sluggish stuff, WD40, pressed
Out of pips that slipped their way in the soil
Of the Bay of Naples fifty years ago

And witched themselves into that silvery upward pour
Of antique, bullet-proof, really goodlooking bark.
    He didn't know he had them,
The guy in the deli. They got pushed together
By some unknown hand in his basement store –

Twin litres of Biba nail-varnish, untouchably
Black and alone. Now he sets them side by side
    On the highest shelf as Ivy Street lights go on,
To preside over tins of Shark Fin Soup,
Almond Parfait Supreme, his Lavender Liquorice Rods.

Here we are, look – alone, a jewelly secret,
Hansel and Gretel in Aladdin's cave of
    Cupressa Dolmades, looking down from the gods
On Banana Conserve and Vintage Marmalade
Plus a Rumpelstiltskin heap of *Farmhouse Gold*.

Never mind tomorrow's big opening, blinds
Flying up on us. Whatever the future holds,
    We've got these pistachio truffles and ruffles,
These rowdy ripples of cranberry vinegar
All to ourselves. Sssh, darling, our night has come.

FIELDS OF GOLD

I THE SWING

You lunge forward, keen
  To have a go
When you spot the rope
  Slung from a willow,

Making a single skein
  With its own reflection. Hope
On the touchline, two
  Lives in one

Hanging over and into the Crimplene
  River. So much
Waiting to happen.
  Perfect, you whisper. Perfect.

II PILOT LIGHT

Palomino country. The midnight rodeo.
Then, 'I've got to get back.' But his sleep
Was sea-rattle and sigh
On a round-pebbled beach
And she was his hold on the sand
Underneath. 'Wake him up. Make him go.'
But each fold and pore of his cheek
In the wash of the lamp, eyelashes at rest

Where there'd be a dash of cleavage if
She wasn't on her back, his trust, weight,
Odysseus exhaustion, said no –
Give us three minutes more. Till she
Was sleep too: weed-swirl, out of depth,
At one with the sea of his breath.

III A LICK AND A PROMISE

. . . leaving your shaving tackle,
That spiral scuff of wooden-soldier blue,
Yellow, green,
The heartline-friendly handle, splay

Of the bristles I so rarely see
That polar-bear your cheekbones every morning,
Abandoned on our New
York basin's luxury mauve lip

As if you'd gone to Washington for a day,
A week, a year, and when you're back
Might kiss me through
Fine flowing handlebars. A Father Christmas leer.

RATTLESNAKES AND RUBIES

We want to see how gems get made in Rio.
How jewel-hunters of Brazil are feather-probing leagues
Of chocolate earth, sifting a mine-wall's sixty-five-foot dance
Of ladder-silhouettes, or filtering mountain streams patrolled
   By mythic venom-pushers like the *fer de lance*
As they lie in wait under fallen logs
For nine (at least) species of frog. We want to see
Rotating knife-wheels, dusted with diamond, release

The voodoo-shine of morganite from ruddy gobs
Of neo-slingshot, learn to tell good ones by comparing them
   To master stones picked out by crystallographers.
We want jewel-surgeons, droves of them, in action,
Making the perfect cut. 'Marquise', 'Brilliante', 'Classic Drop'.

Well, fine: we get the lot. An eyeful of Brazilian tourmaline
In smoke-yellow, rose, grass-green. Citrine, to see off nightmares.
Amethyst, to keep you sober, unhungover, however much
You drink. Emeralds with veins like splitting fern,
   The beaten silk and cyanide of peridot in
Its hibernated state. Pink chrysoprase; the burn
And blood of rubies; diamonds everywhere
Like dandruff. Then we get fed through to Sales –

To Rosa Klebb, the James Bond torturer, and ranks
Of couples who just rolled up like us to take a look,
   And found themselves in second-honeymoon pose
Facing banks of tiger eye that each set you back
Three thousand. All the sparklers; stones men hack

From mountains, squinny and chip at, set in gold, or buy
For women to wear. 'What do you want to see?'
What do you fancy? An amber wedding wreath?
A ruby bed with platinum sheets? That matching pair

Of sapphire watches trimmed
With custard-gold gold leaf?
We're fine, thanks, as we are.
Years, now, we've worn rings we gave each other,

Since that night you turned up with
(You said) a leopardskin bra,
   And smuggled an opal onto my finger, here, instead.
'You're interested in opals?' She shimmies us three trays.
'An opal is like pumice – soft. The flicks of fire,

These points of pink, blue, yellow, green,
Are billions – look – of water drops.
The more there are, more colour in the stone,
The more expensive.' Please. What *are* we doing here
   When we could be in the forest, or a bar?
Getting into opal hierarchies, you spot the really rare one.
Is she open Saturday? Jesus – you'll be asking next
For credit facilities or Euro-cheques. I slither us out

To the jungle's tapestries, wagon wheels of umbrella-fern
Glowing and glancing with rain
   Plus a drum-roll blues from five
(At least) species of frog. Sheer night falls, instantly. Fritz,
Whom we blindly trust (or do we?) heads across the stream

And up the mountain path with two big sticks, poking
Every pile of leaves, every loose and pitch-black rock.
My canvas-and-Velcro sandals (wet, no socks)
Following your Nike trainers Indian file,
   Eros and Psyche under the Telephone Tree
(Whose lianas are ready to brain us), my freezing fingers up
Your sleeve, we sing 'Rose of Tralee', 'Moon River',
To warn the snakes we're here; and hours later, soaking, reach

A blue-tiled hut. The guard mixes sugarcane-husk
Martinis. Doubles. We admire his wall-art –
   Posters of eight local species of *cascavel*
(A.k.a. rattlesnake), each
Of whose bite leaves seven hours to live. Back home in the hotel,

Your PowerBook glistering with ants, the desk-lamp throws
A fan of floating amber from your head around the wall
And Rio roars outside. Alone, dry, safe (amazingly), we're both
Ourselves again. Both writing; both at work
   Above loonily perfect Copacabana Beach
Where little boys, lime-green and glitter-rose,
Play manic soccer in soft sapphire dusk
To an audience of rearing, floodlit, diamond surf.

RUINS OF HOLY ISLAND ON LOUGH DERG

*'I could eat you,' he said. She replied that only lovers and
cannibals talk like that.*
                              Sean O'Faolain, *Lovers of the Lake*

No, not that Lough Derg, the other. Not
    Where your mother, aged sixteen,
Did pilgrim circuits till her bare feet bled,
Then bussed back to the farm, first light
    And kitten-weak – no eating for three days
And still no food till twelve that night –
To smell, four fields away, *her* mother
    Frying scallions. Heaven she couldn't eat.

That pilgrimage, and others – Lourdes, Knock –
    Made her what she was, upholder of the rosary
In Battersea. But she never forgot
That fry-up. Sweet stink
    Of renunciation, of having to be good.

                    ★

This painting is another holy island, and a different lough.
    The one I saw with you at your old garden's end
In Killaloe, standing beside
The gold-splashed apple tree
    In your one-summer student paradise

Of guitars, patchouli, girlfriends, Brian Boru.
    Years on, we slip among the eighteen moons
Of Saturn in each other
Playing father, mother, holy island, child.
    This magic place. You're all I need.
Your arms. The chalice of your face.
Whatever you were, or longed for as
    A rolling-eyed blond kid, is part of me.

                    ★

Like this lake, as gazed at from the real estate
　　Your dad invested in to lure her back to what he ached
For after thirty years away. His earth, his patch
Of Galway sky. Damned if she would. Lough Derg?
　　God no. It was years – five years – before she'd go.

★

Behind that brick-blown ruin, the painter's done
　　A sunset of goodbye. The Isles of not just Galway –
Greece, before it could be free, with everything
Except the gold light, gone.
　　Cloud, mirrored in the lake, as milky as the drop
She hung in her corsage, those nights at the Irish Club.
Sky, the same translucent yellow-grey
　　As prawn-tails in the sushi bar window at Loch Ray.

Raw fish? How things had changed by the time
　　Your dad and mum came back.
I wish they hadn't waited to go home
In London's shadow of shelved objects. I wish
　　Her prayers had worked for him. For them.

★

Would prayers work for us? As our dial moves
　　Through afternoon, I wish I didn't feel
This putting-off we do (whenever can
Whole nights together be OK – the truth –
　　No harm or blame on anyone?)

Is waiting for a wishbone, wishing on
　　A jack-knife moon. Like that pared flick
In the painting's goldwash air.
An air that's blushing where it bellies to the lake

With just her Cinnamon Umber shade
Of lipstick, or the coral she wore to match her hair:
Still flame, still sunset-bright, that year
    They had back home before he died.

THE STONE THAT FLOWS

A life-time of redheaded allegiance to the Pope
And she lost her faith on the morphine drip
   In Galway Hospital.
From the canteen phone, you told me she was losing all
She'd lived by. What was God
   Worth, and His saints, on a bed
Of dangling oxygen?

Only days to go, the doctors said,
And she was crying down that Great Good Bet
   On seeing you all again,
Cracking her Fabergé egg
Of glass, the stone that flows –
   Her trust in God's own guarantee
Of treasure that can't rust – to ruby smithereens.

I couldn't sleep, that month, couldn't do a thing
But worry about you. The polar bear were moving south.
   One night – get this – I even banged
On Westminster Abbey door, looking for a way back in
For her. That pile of stones so old each one had grown
   Into the other's crevices
Was bolted up in iron and electronics.

But there was light, above a verger's bell.
The House of Commons church:
   Protestant, not Catholic, but – hell . . .
What was I doing? What would I tell them when
They came? A priest showed up
   Behind the frosted glass
Toughened against another night beneath Big Ben.

It wasn't his, that church, but he took me in.
He turned on all the lights he knew about,
   Filled side-chapels with shadow, knelt me down

As if this happened every day: women landing on him
During parish conference (or at cards, I couldn't tell)
    With his sacerdotal mates, asking for miracles
In someone else's mother's mind.

He prayed for her to find
Her faith again. That it'd be OK
    For her, for you.
'Do you want a blessing?' Yup.
You bet I do. I want the works.
    And on my knees beside him in that church
That wasn't his – well, I prayed too.

THE PHOENIX

Her once-red head locked
In a tank of steam.
   Her face, foxing down into nothing
Saying, 'All my beauty's gone.'
She's holding on

To your wrist, your bare arm,
Through a shock hedge of wiring, spliced
   Every which way to intestines,
And rationing herself to Seven-Up
(Plus morphine) on the rocks.

So cold, under the striplight
Night after night
   Through all the carry-ons:
The bubble-cloud of rosaries,
The small-hours foraging for ice

In the hospital kitchen. But so proud
Of this big cuckoo she
   Brought into the world, as you
Sang with her, day after glary day,
All the words of all the Jim Reeves songs

Or any you rustled up between you,
Anything anyone there could sing about –
   'Tipperary', 'Star of the Sea' –
To ease that inward
Journey, launch her out.

'THE OLD BOG ROAD'

I wanted you to cry for her
  With arms that loved you round you,
Somebody's shoulders – mine, for preference –

Filling your new ache of nothing there,
  And yes, my fingers steadying vertebrae
In the furrow of your spine

Where they always do, above your trouser waist.
  As you got through every verse
Of the song she used to sing, my bronze

Fridge humming along with its 'Dress
  Botticelli's Venus in Jeans and Bikini'
Magnets, your face

Was a Wash 'n' Go ad baptizing my hair. A flash flood
  You dried, being you, on the nearest available
Dog's mud-skittered Dri-Bag.

ARSON

(After Apollonius of Rhodes)

He strung his bow and lifted from the quiver
An arrow he'd never shot, a messenger
Of fever. Gliding up to Jason,

He fiddled till he got the arrow settled
In the middle of the string, then slowly
Chasmed his hands apart and shot Medea.

She sat there stunned while Eros laughed,
Flashing out from the high-roofed hall,
Leaving the arrow in her heart. Smouldering:

The sudden start of flame. Her soul gave in
To its melting pain, going up
Like the handful of twigs a woman nests

Round a single coal.
A woman straight from fairy-tale
Whose task is spinning wool.

She lights her tiny fire
When she wakes on her own, in the dark.
Flames jet from the spark to swallow all

Her kindling in one go.
So Eros the Destroyer took Medea's heart
And burnt her up in secret.

GEISHA

Call it raw silk: the lotus-and-narcissus
Shadow-whites or scumbled cream
   Of the Embassy's Full Moon Drawing Room
   Where you shock everyone
By getting the Attaché's wife (one hand
Before her mouth) to dally with you behind a screen

Of *washi* paper made in Imadate, West Japan,
In the precinct of Kakui the Paper God
   Where votive ribbons, zig-zag paper lightnings, jig
   And flitter from the temple pediment like a fringe
Of torn-up letters, and the family firm of Heyzaburo
Dye their pulp, then thin it to translucent mousseline.

'If she'd had a fan,' you say,
'She'd have giggled behind that too.'
   You go home on the silver-paper wheels
   Of a Tokyo-registered Rolls Royce Phantom Nine
With your other partner in her grey
Crushed-velvet Issey Miyake,

To the separate rooms she's insisted on
Ever since you shared a home. Next night
   I watch you lay out geisha arts
   To do the giggle, charm me too with your aplomb
At passing the long white
Hours we're apart.

VOODOO SHOP

Take the fortune-teller in white lace
Whose brown, fat-flowing upper arm
  Is punched to bruised-plum black.
  She holds my hand palm-up on scrambly satin
  At her stall in the cobbled cul-de-sac
Behind the Slave Museum – whose logo is another girl,
Venerada da Igreja Da Rosario, R.J.,
  The saint with a padlocked mouth so she won't say
  How she was whipped to death. Our sibyl
  Is from Bahia, North Brazil.
She doesn't look your way, not a breath
Or glance though you're at my side, a strict Papa

At the big school interview. Yet when she tells
My fortune what she sees is you –
  The Mighty Hunter, striding through
  The forest with his bow, making the whole earth tremble
  As he goes. And I, the Lady of Monsoon and Fire, must lay
Three sweeties in our garden back at home
So the Children (whoever *they* are) will protect you,
  And bury a large wax key at your place of work.
  The sacred sea-shells say this will connect you
  To prosperity. That's where it's at. My life is your career
And Oxum, Goddess of Success, shall smile on it.
She doesn't know we'll never have a garden of our own

Except for here. I'm all for looking after you.
I'll slip three toffees nicked from last night's bar
  Under tree-roots on the sea-front sweep of our hotel
  So Rio de Janeiro's spirit-waifs will keep you safe
  As amber. I give up, though, on smuggling wax keys
To an IBM-compatible Macintosh
On the eighteenth floor
  Of centrally-heated, open-plan Canary Wharf.

But your voodoo blood is up now: you want more.
Feathers and candles, powders
That work magic in the dark like phosphorus crystals
Blush-encrusting photographic glass,

And smoky jewelled vials marked
'Come Here To Me' in Gothic script.
　　We bowl through sleepy grey backstreets,
　　Closing shutters for siesta, till we find
　　The city's secret — voodoo Harrods.
Barrow-loads of wax, red-headed pins
And greeny-black cock-feathers, plus the full
　　Cast of the Tarot. Staring figures, three feet high
　　In shot-silk robes, the soft blue mould
　　Of centuries down every fold.
The Knights of Hell are here, swords blobbed
With lozenges of ruby glass,

Horned umber devils with magenta claws,
Angels on silver wings in locked glass cases,
　　Questing Kings on palfreys, Queens
　　With tinsel faces, nipples glimmering
　　Through snowy gauze like cherries
In ice-cream. Beelzebub; jungle gods of Amazon;
Mary Magdalen; the Priest of Saul.
　　Symbols to die for. Freud, Jung and the I Ching
　　Would have a ball. So who or what
　　Do you fancy now we're here? Love spells?
We've got all those already, for ourselves.
Sir Lancelot, the Queen of Spades . . .

I'll buy you who you really want: the Charmer, a white-
Haired anecdotalist and singer. Your voodoo
　　Alter ego — no, you simply like
　　His operating skills, the way he sits at dinner
　　Schmoozing women, patrons, friends.
Does how we see ourselves depend

On me and you, or on these voodoo djinns?
    You buy me Brown Girl, a sleeping leopard
    Plumped against her shin, a daggery belt
    Of feathers round her groin. Alone, intent on distance,
Hoping – what? To melt into cloud-forest
With the sambur and the katydids; join

The Mighty Hunter, his all-seeing eyes? Is that how I am
With you, a flickery deciduous disguise
    Of jungle cryptograms from Salvador to Iguaçu
    To Bogotá? Or is she longing to belong, this girl,
    To the Charmer's wine-bar world of Prada slingbacks,
Infidelities, and knowing the words to all the seventies hits?
Does who I am depend on who you are?
    You want to keep your cake at home
    And eat it in the woods with me. What am I doing in Brazil,
    Or in this role at all?
Where's the Lady of Monsoon and Fire
Got to; and which do I want to be? You say. Your call.

THE GRIEF MAPS

You find the manuals ('How to Mourn')
On Borders' Self-Help shelves.
'Imagine this to be your Trail Guide in a park.
The paths available from Point Death

'Are Numbness, Shock, Denial.
They lead to Loneliness, Confusion,
Visions of dark lorries speeding, nose to tail
On the M25, each with a hole in its black side

'Like the last piece missing from a jigsaw,
Or sable ice-bergs calving
In the Sea of Desolation.
This is where hallucinations start –

'The hand on your arm from behind
As you enter a room.
Expect a second goodbye,
Probably in a dream. Then you arrive

'At Sunset Point, that canyon lip
Of apricot and rose,
Best place to overlook
Those Lemsip table-lands

'You now can call the past.
Or Mount Cayambe, sole spot on the globe
Where temperature
And latitude reach zero both at once.'

What the books don't say
Is how you then discover
You never felt he loved you.
That hand on your arm would be a first.

Not true to life as you have lived it.
Think, instead, of how he sent you to a shrink
When you were eight, or nine.
Shrinks, for anyone in the business,

Were the only panacea.
He had your IQ tested, you were fine –
Too fine, in fact – but shy, withdrawn;
Bereft in the midst of plenty.

Maybe one night you tell your lover
All the details, soaking his chest with tears;
Then find your naked body curling,
As he sleeps, in some weird

Torture of its own behind a curtain
To a window looking down on rainy dawn
In, let's say, Dublin. Merrion Square.
He wakes up, sighs – he wants to do this right –

And scoops you back to bed. He's suddenly seen
How easy desolation is. How quick and near,
This place he's never been, or not like this. Despair
Has a different compass-point for him.

The way he's angry, talks about abuse,
Is summertime. You suddenly see how mad
It was, a dad who didn't seem,
Whatever went on inside himself, to know or like

You much (except your brain)
And yet kept tabs
On you by paying someone else. A woman spy,
A thief of dreams, with Viennese cake

For tea on paper doilies.
It seemed the normal father thing

To have you walk that daily post-school drag
To her, from buses going on

To Maida Vale, Wood Green,
Past hedges of two-tone holly
And pavements with pink edges
Where small bricks slid in the rain.

No reason given why,
If you tried to throw warm water in the air,
It came down ice. The manuals don't say
That only by retracing that blank wilderness

With no map but your head, now safe
On your boyfriend's arm,
Do you see what love is up for. Then imagine
He goes too, and you're alone.

SURF RAGE AT BONDI BEACH

'There are a lot of guys out there,'
   He said into the mike
With London on the line,
   'Fighting for waves and the right of way
On waves. More arguments over waves
   Than there are waves.

'Wave-riding is . . . competitive.
   You can't forget the lane code –
Whoever's nearest to the breaking
   Of the wave, has got the right
To it. This guy dropped, mid-wave,
   In front of another guy! Incredible!

'Too right there was a fight. Too bad
   He died. It's a big deal out there –
Waves like tornadoes on the sun,
   Men's bodies small and light on them,
Raging to ride them home.
   Surfers get very possessive of their waves.'

At evening he went back to be alone
   On the empty shore, the Kaahumanu board
Under his right arm – a levitating shark,
   Pointing a shimmery snout where it belonged,
At ocean – in a khaki light dull-shot
   With silver where little zig-zags (left by waves

That came and crashed and conquered, got
   Themselves fought about,
Then slid to puddled nothing) still held water
   In all that open, democratic sand.
So lit today, so talked about
   Over the world's air-waves.

And now, with surfers, media, sunlight
    Gone, and twilight's roc wing darkening
Slight hillocks, flattened scuffings
    Of the sand, his own reflection underpins
Him black and upside down
    Like one of Plato's shadows –

The one survivor of the Truth come back
    To tell the tale – lugging a giant
Feather, crossbar to his torso, long
    As he is tall. Even the upright
Body is a shadow now, waving and
    Drowning in the has-been-gold of land.

SHAPING UP

This is the sanding room for Bosendorfer Grands
Where Tori Amos and her Manager are looking for
   The perfect instrument on which she may,
   At last, wrap up her song about the night in LA
She was raped. (Some loser with a gun.)
The only way she'll get real again, get past
   Her favourite red silk number from Monsoon
   Ripped apart on the ass of a Plymouth.
'What's music for, in anyone?' her PR says, when asked.
'To give a shape to pain.'

So what does Tori meet, where the hallowed instruments
Get made? Piped melodies, rained above the noise
   Like any factory. Boys
   Yomping saffron curls of raw mahogany.
Grands need a lot of space, and everywhere Tori looks
Are twenty-five-foot walls with shots of naked girls,
   Legs wide. Why the dodgy ambience, such a high-
   Class place? 'These photographs provide
Inspiration to our workers in their delicate task,
Creating the body of the piano,' says the guide.

A SHORT HISTORY OF DARKNESS

I TALES OF THE JUNGLE

When you lift your gin and tonic
In the dug-out canoe at dusk,
    Relieved to get away on a PR trip
Down the Amazon,

Almost upon
You, checking out the musk
    From your left foot
(Plus, I hope, my *Jungle Formula*

Mosquito Milk), where the still uncut
Big toe-nail pushes through your favourite
    Paul Smith silk
'Tequila Sunrise'

Sock, are the citron mini-rainbows
With that liquorice kick
    At centre
Of a cayman's eyes.

II THE WITNESS

Last night in a dream
    She saw her mother's engagement ring.
    A tiger agate
Wrapped in a small gold snake

That had lost its diamond eyes
    In the vale – I mean
    Along the line – of fifty years
Of marriage; children; widowing.

III TOUCAN TREE

At the still eye of the storm
When she'd lost hope
Of Zacatecan silver mines
And chaos was a rope-burn in her throat,

She took out the toucan tree he'd given her
On their last day in Rio,
The cherry-bud occupants, bead-bright
As an inventory of therapeutic gems,

Hanging from emerald wire
On separate stems,
And positioned it dead centre in the new, off-white
Carrara fireplace of her empty room,

Cold as it was
And pink-brick innocent of fire.

HOT ASH

for Sarah

I'm glad you've come through.
I hadn't seen you since your father died –

And mine. The bar was lined
With friends. I'd split up after four years

With my lover – or maybe not –
Yes definitely. Burnt, poor bugger,

By fall-out from whatever mourning is.
He couldn't take how it took me. But you

Were sparkling, glowing-eyed,
And thinking about flowers. Your garden side.

Veronica, jasmine, aquilegia,
Pennyroyal. 'Are you OK?' I asked.

'I'm coming out of it,' you said. 'And you?'
'I think I'm going into it.'

Gins and tonic, ice and lemon,
Glittered on the bar.

'Yesterday,' I said, 'I made a fire.
Cleared dog shit off the grass,

'Pulled rotten stumps, burnt everything
I didn't need. Dead peach tree, black-spot

'Roses, crumbling trellis, sodden gate.
Even today, the ashes are too hot

'For rubbish bins,
Too hot to spread on plants.

'But *your* dad, Sarah – did he love
You? Did you have all that?' Your face lit,

And your voice. You looked great.
'I *was* loved – unconditionally.'

You'd come through as you said,
And come out stronger. Me –

What I've got in my garden this wet spring
Is poison ivy. Agrimony

I must have planted and forgotten.
Hellebore

That hadn't seen the light of day before.
I must get rid of them.

THE LIGHT THAT CASTS A SHADOW

So this was it. The dark star, death star, end
   Of world. And we were dinosaurs
On either side a six-mile-deep divide
   Where Himalayas bubbled up
From Earth's rose-red inside.

Try strangling that blazing ball of gas
   We call the sun, compress
Its eight-hundred, sixty-four thousand miles
   Till all the atoms smash
And run,

And it's a white dwarf, weighing in
   At a tinkly thirty-thousand-mile diameter.
Contract the thing again
   Till all electrons melt and nothing's left
But neutrons. What you've got's a neutron star,

A sun nine miles across. The only thing
   That can escape from it is light –
But light that's struggling, baby. Go on, do
   The shrink again, till neutrons collapse too.
What's left is three miles wide. A skating rink.

You could walk it in forty minutes, easy.
   But escape velocity, the minimum speed
That'd lift you off its gravity, has passed
   The speed of light. Nothing's getting out
Except black-body radiation, cabling back an SOS

To our lost universe: a sable Very pistol
   Shooting from any object
That happens to fall in. If you dropped by, you'd be
   At once an elongated I, a ribbon of molten bees.
The closer in you got, the thinner you'd be squeezed.

There – that's the gravity of black holes.
   So nuclear, so greedy-dark,
You'd never have time to register
   Its Gorgon-gaze as black.
That's it. That's where we were. A soup

Of valedictory X-rays. Quantum cryptography,
   All chaos and lost light,
But different for each of us. For you,
   The hell of neutral. Everything losing edge
And colour; a no-man's-mashed-potato-land of night.

No silhouettes or *chiaroscuro*. Rays have to hit
   The retina for that, and you'd seen every light go out.
As for me, I walked about like a Polo filled with smoke.
   A zombie, whose soul had been extracted and exhumed
To tell of poisoning by a *vaudoux* sorcerer,

Adept in the toxic bite of puffer fish.
   Or like a Spix Macaw, the only living thing
That spoke the language of a wiped-out Indian tribe,
   Who'd seen her mate, the last recorded of her species,
Killed for his pure blue feathers. But

We followed separate down-paths to the same dead sun
   Where somehow, under some astro masterplan,
We stumbled on a switch
   We had to thump three times, so halogen
Could well against the cliff

In rose-petal coronas, scattering feathers
   Of translucency like photons riding shotgun
On a rainbow, warning us
   'There is no meaning in your lives,
And no life in your hearts, without each other.'

Even the wires of tension-calibrated steel
    Joined in
Saying, 'Look, you two. You're very far
    From perfect. This is no solar idyll
You've got here. There's muddle – sin,

'If you like to call it that – inside you both. Earth spins
    On its tilted axis;
The light you know each other by
    Will keep on changing. Yet the source is still
What they used to say God is.

'Knowledge. Love. The rays that give this world
    Its ticking filaments and edge.
Light that matters on the stage
    Is light that casts a shadow.
Better now? That freeze-your-marrow night

'All over? You both feel
    Winter's gone? You've got the dazzle
Back, full working order? Fine. But it's the Fall
    Sweethearts, the dark,
That'll keep you real.'

PLANE TRAIL AT CANNES

... is white ink, writing fishbones on the crazy-paving sky
Above this glitter-pink harbour, scribbling over whorls
Of grey cloud delicate as the stitched and puckered seam
Between your balls – a gene determined by

Your dad, or your mother's dad, and back
Through generations we couldn't count if we lay
In bed like this all day, my head along your thigh,
My fingertips
Feathering the secret ocean ridges of your skin

Like that dog, a stray, who found her ideal home
And hid discarded pizza cartons in the crypt
Of the holiest church in Christendom,
Then licked her black lips gently as she slept.

JOINERY

'Harmony: from Greek *harmottein*, to fit together'
Universal English Dictionary

You try and hide the tears
High-tailing it round your cheekbones
When I put Bob Marley on, but I know they're there
And why. 'Redemption Songs':

That bare guitar, pitchforking the idea
Of harmonizing having nothing
Into the kitchen, into our lives,
And saying to your PowerMac,

Just plugged in, the chanterelles
And litre of Gordon's Gin
You bought, 'But song is all I am.
Plucked strings; and my voice asking yours

To join in.' The one surviving thing,
More powerful than any silencer:
The head of Orpheus pitched downriver,
Refusing not to sing.

Think pianos, wrecked beyond repair –
The upright, grand, and overstrung
Going in to the infill tip.
Removal men love doing it, says Lenny.

'Normally we have to take such care
And the buggers are so heavy.'
Or the Nazi general who listed in his memoir all
The musical instruments his men smashed –

The first thing, he explained, that soldiers everywhere
Tear into, at the looting signal.

'Yan-Luo Cloud-Gongs, China.
Udu Pots of rattan and red clay

'That hum the note on which the world began,
Nigeria. A hundred-year-old Kora, steel
And sandalwood, from Senegal.
In Java, a Soran Slen Tem,

'Jade-green and black in dragon shape,
Carrying on its back the bells of Heaven.'
All whacked against the wall or snapped
Under regulation heels. 'Mars,' he wrote

(He had an old-style education),
'Is the enemy of Apollo.'
But some sounds – see the trumpet
Buried with Tutankhamun but still playable –

Never die. In the general's cell, the chords
From recarved, glued, revarnished shells
Of lutes and viols, tabrets, tambourines,
Steal back in dreams to hum his soul to hell.

And at sunset on the bypass, when flies
Have left the infill site and building rubble lies
Six feet above the charcoal and manila
Piano lids and ivories,

They say you can stand on London clay
As twilight falls on no-man's-land
Of next-to-motorway, and hear harmonics
Creep from below the ground

To Pegasus and the nebulae of circumpolar stars.
As for you with your slug of gin, afraid
Your tears are facile, even fake (a word that's flung
At you often enough): I take everything you say you feel

On trust. For me as I peel Safeways Moroccan spuds,
You've conjured Orpheus in this kitchen
This shadow place you call
Your second home. But it's not only song

That does it. No one note on another,
No chord progression promising like a lover
(Or Ryanair's logo), 'Take Me, I'm Yours,
I'm Giving All I Am', stays buried long.

YOU, SHIVA, AND MY MUM

Shall I tell how she went to India
At the age of eighty
For a week in the monsoon

   Because her last unmarried son
   Was getting married to a girl
   With a mask of yellow turmeric on her face

At the shrine of Maa Markoma
In the forest where Orissa's last
Recorded human sacrifice took place?

   How this mother of mine rode a motorbike,
   Pillion, up a leopard-and-leeches path
   Through jungle at full moon,

Getting off to shove away
The sleeping buffalo,
Puddled shaves of sacred calf?

   How she who hates all frills
   Watched her feet painted scarlet henna,
   Flip-flop pattern between the toes

And backward swastikas at heel, without a murmur?
How she climbed barefoot to Shiva
Up a rock-slide – where God sat

   Cross-legged, navy blue,
   On a boulder above his cave,
   One hand forbidding anyone impure,

Or wearing leather, to come in?
How she forded Cobra River
In a hundred degrees at noon

40

To reach the God's familiar — his little bull of stone,
A pinky blaze of ribbons, bells, hibiscus —
And, lifelong sceptic that she is,

The eyes of all the valley on her — Tribal, Hindu,
Atheist and Christian — bowed? Shall I tell how you
Laughed fondly at me for my pride

In her? How I wait on the miracle
Of your breath in my ear? Shall I tell
Them? Yes. Tell that.

HOME COOKING

You spread our Free Range Duck
Breasts with your trade-mark mix

Of honey, soya, Chinese Five Spice
While I etch
A fingernail down your spine

Ending in a fuck
The length of our kitchen table

Making the bread-board rise
To its feet, the dog beneath us whine,
And Sainsbury's poultry burn.

BUTTERFLY LANDING ON A PAINTING BY BRIDGET RILEY

The soul is a fugitive and wanderer, driven by the decrees and laws of gods.

Plutarch, *De exilio*

I SWALLOWTAIL

Suppose you're walking on a cliff-top
Back where you used to live, in Greece.
The island where your friend Kay,
Who's dying in an Athens flat of emphysema
On a round-the-clock line of oxygen, grew up.
There's nothing to be done. You've flown to see her
Twice. You'll go again.
Unstoppable cicadas, hot-resin smell
Of pines. The sweat – you've forgotten how it rivulets
Between the breasts, how wet is constant.
Sea. Cream-turquoise halogen, or luminous green silk
Spread out below to archipelagos
Of rocks and nibbled inlets. Islands, islands: milk
Opalescent shivers and frills at every edge.

Suppose a stripy butterfly, black-white
Albino tartan, large as a hand, appears stage right
As you're walking up the road to a brandy-snap
Red beach, to find your daughter and her friend
In snorkels, Factor Twenty-Five, and Aqua Babe
Sarongs. You stop, for this unfolded scrap
Of animate origami
Haunting orange clods of earth
Below the olives. Eyelash antennae;
Proboscis, siphoning honey you can't see:
It settles by you like an omen, zebra wings outspread
On a tiny, dusty, pink-yellow flowerhead. Some vetch
(Your mother would know the Latin
Name) at the empty road's pale edge.

Imagine this has been a terrible year for death,
Loss, all-gone-wrongs. The bull-waves' neuron glitter
Leaps the cliff. Swallows on a clef
Of italic phone wire dab their next
Month's leaving-song over noon sky's indigo razzle.
A pop request you sang with Nikos years ago
Bellies from 'Antigone Hotel' pool stereo.
I zoe, i zoe san chelidoni,
Fevgi ap ta cheili mou. 'Life like a breath,
Like a swallow, is leaving, is fleeing, my lips.'
Suppose your dad had taught you ancient Greek,
The key to all of this. Blue sea. Friends.
The sparkling, stupidly gorgeous islands.
Even the daughter. Songs.

Suppose you're looking for a way to remember him well.
He could only be what he was. His gift was black OK,
But made you want to learn, find new things, tell
About them. With his bride's relations adept in
Botany, or ornithology, he got up for her
A knowledge they didn't have: lepidoptera.
This specimen has popped into the olive grove for him.
He loved, by teaching what he loved, and he loved
Greece. Ruins, moths of the psyche, language, myth.
Those are the things in him that led you here.
Back-tracking twenty years, you remember seeing him off
At Athens Airport. How his eyes behind their glasses
(The irises' circumference, like yours, darker than the rest)
Had filled, amazingly, with tears.

II RAIN

A sudden squall of rain in the piazza. It's 1960. Venice.
    The dark girl, knocking back Camparis with her lover
(Old enough to be her dad; the centre of everything she is),

Has won a prize. She's twenty-nine, all go,
And flirting with Hard Edge
   Abstractionism. He thinks she's difficult, and young.
They're splitting up. She doesn't know.

Together, they've explored the Futurists.
   They tried to visit Gino Severini,
Futurism's founder, but he won't be seen, he's
   Ill. Now she's drawing on the table, arguing.
'Shapes that flow
   Through space destroy the world as you and I
Perceive it.' But her voice is shrill.

He's playing teacher, lecturing on
   The inner life of colour. She's saying, too
Loud and wrong, somehow,
   That losing certainty of line could change
Things for a painter, rearrange him, set him free
   (She still says 'he'), 'or whisk
Him off to places he never dreamed he'd see.'

You can hear how young – you want to fold her in
   Your arms, make her slow down –
But you love the flinging out: the risk.
   More Camparis. He forgives
The arguing for now; until they're home.
   What she's really up to
Is watching how rain turns

All this Renaissance paving – midnight geometry
   Of star and parallelogram, black granite set
In milkstone from the cold Carrara ridge –
   To a swirl of snake-skin
Runnels. Chaos physics.
   In herself, only half-aware, she's marvelling
How a thing that seemed so certain

Can in a flash, a moment, fall to bits. She's no idea
    This will change the way we see.
Rain stops – the flagstones dry – that pristine, seven-
    Point clarity comes back. But her eyes have taken in
How pattern, safe curtain
    Of the given world, can buckle, go
Molten on you, disappear.

Afterwards, she'll see it everywhere, a witchy spell
    On pell-mell dying leaves
Or zebra crossings over Russell Square,
    And sloping glass of a Ford Popular's rear window
Where it slippingly reflects
    The dark-pale-dark of bedrooms in Imperial Hotel.
It'll stay with her, unnoticed, when he's left.

III KISS

He's gone. She can't believe it, can't go on.
She's going to give up painting. So she paints
Her final canvas, total-turn-off
    Black. One long
    Obsidian goodbye.
A charcoal-burner's Smirnoff,
The mirror of Loch Ness
Reflecting the monster back to its own eye.

But something's wrong. Those mad
Black-body particles don't sing
Her story of despair, the steel and
    Garnet spindle
    Of the storm.
This black has everything its own sweet way.
Where's the I'd-like-to-kill-you
Conflict? Try once more, but this time add

46

A curve to all that straight. And opposition –
White. She paints black first. A grindstone belly
Hammering a smaller shape
    Beneath a snake
    Of in-betweening light.
'I feel like this. I hope that you do, too.
Black crater. Screw you. *Kiss.*'
And sees a voodoo flicker, where two worlds nearly touch

And miss. That flash, where white
Lets black get close, that dagger of not-quite contact,
Catspaw panic, quiver on the wheat
    Field before thunder –
    There. That's it.
That's her own self, in paint,
Splitting what she was from what she is.
As if everything that separates, unites.

IV SHIFT

Leaving rage behind,
    She's found herself painting
Movement. Painting beyond
    The frequency where retinas respond,
Painting black-white isotopes
    Of Colbalt 57. Painting REM in action, climax heaven.
As if a cart-load of leucistic leopards
    Had colonized her heart,
She's painting optical-illusion cracks
    In how we view the universe.
Out in, up down, lose win.

Suppose my butterfly
    With innocent smashed-eggshell wings,
Should flicker in on all these canvases
    Called things like *Fission, Blaze, Uneasy Centre, Drift.*

How would it feel, a cut-out paper ghost weighed down
    By schizophrenic molecules; these stark,
Electric, black-white shifts
    Of noticing and soul I'm asking it
To stand for — what my dad thought and did,
    And what I thought of him? At home
In just that instability and rift.

V SEND-OFF

So all this liminal
    Black and white
        Was saying goodbye
To him? I'm doing it with you
    Beside me, a hundred miles away

But listening in. Not on the mobiles —
    Neither of us has a clue
        About a 'Roaming' menu. Rays
Showering tumours in the brain
    Are no good here. I'm on Kay's

Island (still Kay's island), laid
    Like Homer's shield
        On the misty sea. You're in
A renovated tower from 'Maltese Holidays'.
    But over these salty, sweaty, blue-feather miles, I feel

Your heart beat, almost touch
    The breastbone that upset
        You, age eleven,
When your dad came home with Johnson's Chest
    Expander. A steel-spring Waterloo. Your Armageddon.

Four settings: you couldn't manage more
    Than one. The thing snapped shut

And guillotined blue pyjama buttons
Pinging them across the floor.
    You gave up. Now you say

There's a hollow in your chest
    You could hold a party in.
        Seems fine to me. From my
Current bearings in the Mediterranean, I
    Thank Christ for the whole thing.

                    ★

When summer's over, you'll surprise
    Me with a ring
        You're buying, now, among
The pizza-parlours and boutiques
    Of Valletta's cassia-scented blond backstreets.

Baltic amber, set in silver, just the goldspray
    Green-beneath-the-skin
        Of this Ionian, slubbed-
Silk sea. You'll give it to me
    Looking in my eyes

As anxiously –
    Did something bad get in
        There, while you were away? –
As a wolf recovering
    Its cub.

                    ★

It's not deserved,
    This joining that began
        On red-as-Gauguin Devon earth
And waltzes on
    Through jungle, quicksand, desert.

Balloons that found their moorings in
　　Each other, a whole new nebula
　　　In heaven
You'd never think
　　They *could* have found, those two;

Relief
　　At hearing each other's voice
　　　As ludicrous and final as the 'Ah!'
Ham actors do
　　On radio, when they drink.

　　　　　　　★

Because of all you've given, and keep giving – wild
　　As Tibetan tigers on the Wheel of Life,
　　　Gentle as ten-pence pieces under the pillow
Swapped at night
　　For the milk-tooth of a sleeping child, and bright

As the Greek word *aiolos*, which means
　　Goldflash, wind-skimmer, quickbeam
　　　And flicker-light,
Hot-surface radiant, moccasin-sheeny, blazoned
　　And skew-curve with white-gleam – I can say

That was his soul I met out there, in the dazzle
　　Of Lixouri Bay.
　　　Hanging,
A moment, over ice-cream wrappers,
　　Baby bindweed, take-away

Grease-tissue from kebabs,
　　And Loutraki-water empties
　　　Glittering half-hidden
In a ditch by the stony kerb.
　　Then open wings above the sea

To the hard-earned phosphorous burn
   Of a Greek horizon. Free now, forgiven,
     Out from under Athena's olive tree.
Looking for more to give, his way,
   And more to learn.

SCARLET LADY

She knows. After all these years. Your turquoise phone
Quacking the Mexican Hat Dance to an empty room
Like a duck that's laid an egg, to tell the world
I'd left a message, has a lot to answer for.

At least she doesn't know I'm here with you today,
This flat in the Vieux Carré,
Walls heaving with Spanish Moss for insulation,
On the white and blue new-minted thoroughfare

Where Tennessee Williams wrote
A Streetcar Named Desire.
No cupboards. Hooks fell off the wall
When you hung up my silk blouse,

The oven nearly gassed us. But it's ours,
The only home we'll ever own together,

For a week. We don't know
What's going to happen. I couldn't love you so
Blue-fire upsettingly
If I wasn't sure you love your children more.

It wouldn't *be* love, in my book,
If I thought you could give up what you adore
Or if I brought myself to wish you would.
Still, just for now, we're in a last-ditch heaven.

Dawn spray of hoses, washing down this run
Of lace-iron bra-and-knicker colonnades
And balconies in painted filigree
On Bourbon Street, is foamy muslin

Curtaining blowing sunlight as we walk.
But me, I'm frightened of the scarlet doll you bought

As a voodoo souvenir.
You and your magic. How you're drawn to it:
The whole idea of one small elixir
And – *pouf* – the world's alright,

You've got away with what you wanted, reality
Won't strike. And you conjure up, as only you
Can do, narcoleptic roses of the night
To bloom all round us. But despite

The thin-skinned, sparkly, Mississippi light,
Or the pair of us dancing everyone off the floor
To a gold guitar playing 'Voodoo Child'
Top-speed in a midnight bar,

Here on our sofa is this stitchy doll. A tourist thing
In plastic packaging. 'Goddess of Evil'. Small. Red felt.

A kid could sew it. Nothing like the dirty staring scrap
Of calico and flax with 'Leave Her, Come to Me'
Scribbled over her outstretched arms on a shelf
In the Drug Museum, among ads for goatskin

Condoms (what was *that* like?), rusted tins
Of Ague Tonic, Snake-Bite Kit, Kickapoo Indian Tea,
And rows of stoppered bottles – 'Devil's Drawing Powder',
'Johnson's Conquer Root', and 'Take Me, Lover'.

Did spoiling spells and love potions do their stuff?
Even your imitation could be real enough.
This is the way, if there's a will. I've read
'Instructions' stapled to the label, terrified

She'll sniff it out when you get back, among the clothes
I've loved you in this week (maybe this cobalt shirt

Of yours, the one you buttoned me into against November cold)
From the fibreglass valise we bought you in New York
Four years ago. She's already left notes for you in there.
'Put Down That Drink.' 'Get Back to Work.'

They're lying on the floor like spying snow,
Like sycamore seed-wings, bleached. Hard not to feel
They're poisoned, seeing how she tried to deal
With her lover's wife. But that's not fair.

I mustn't think like that. We're all *in extremis* here
Or will be soon. Honey, I'm scared she'll hang
This moppet in her cupboard in the dark.
And then, at midnight, bang the pins in its red felt heart

So our always love, that never meant to hurt,
Will disappear.

ON TREMBLE ISLAND

'I loved him,' said the small tornado
From her golden lectern in the void
To the expert in the life-cycle of whirlpools.

What did he care? He was measuring
Shock-waves caught by time-lapse video
On Tremble Island. His study was

The vortex and the seismograph,
The glassy keloid scars
Of waters when they clash

In a Grade A maelstrom. Our tornado's fading
To a whisper now, but she persists.
'I loved what was inside him – and still is,

'Though I'll never open that file again.
Inner gloss on the vulture's wing,
The caught-flare, split-clod flash

'Of deep-dug clay. Never mind the way he'll blame
Me, now he's lost me; now he's hurt.
In my body, such as it is, and in my soul

'I gave him home he'd never known
Before, and won't again. I've been
His fox earth, full moon, whiskey at two a.m.

'In a tumbler ringed like the Cats-Eye Nebula
With concentric trails of poppy-rose, a hair-
Line rim of green,

'And we were the two stars at the core, so close
We breathed and thought one air.
I loved his Arabic calligraphy

'Of messages on my mobile
Flicked from a Soho carpark in the dark –
"I love you beyond anything I've dreamed."

'What'll he have to sustain
Him now, on that Medusa hearth
Where children tread broken glass

'On the kitchen floor, and meteorites
Hurl silence at each other
In knots of high-speed flame?'

CASABLANCA AND THE CHILDREN OF STORM

Concerning flight. You mustn't say 'migrate'
For journeys you don't come back from.

Radar operators
Picking up echoes from migrating birds, write

'Angels' in the logbook
Because they come unbidden.

Migrating birds belong
To the school of night.

Their licking silhouettes, drawn on
For hours across the moon

By a magnetism you might,
If it were us, call faith,

Keep going
On a butterball of gold fat, glowing

In the breast like a secret love
Where clavicle and wishbone fuse.

Silk-gristle wings,
So easily blown off-course

Or blagged by hawks and guns
In blue-blush-ivory dawn

At crossing-points of continents.
Gibraltar, Bosporos, Camargue:

What makes them (and what makes us)
Hurl their capillaries out

To life-or-death adventure?
Outside things –

High winds,
A drop in temperature,

The dying of summer flies and autumn seed –
Or inner need?

★

Skellig Michael, off the coast
Of Kerry – I saw it on my own,

We never went south, did we, you and I,
Those times we had in Ireland –

Is the naked summer home
Of shearwaters, and shy

Chocolate-feathered guillemots.
Baby dodos, as drawn by Edward Lear.

Both fly
Six thousand air-miles, Kerry

To South America and back, each year.
But superstars of homing, and fidelity,

Are smallest of all web-footed birds,
The storm petrels. They dangle their feet Christ-fashion

When they skim the peaking surfaces of waves
After microscopic prey, as if they walked on water.

Fishermen call them Little St Peter, Peterell.
One for you, love, who whisper 'Sacred Heart!'

And 'Mother of God!' in passion
Or when you feel, as you hate to feel, afraid.

Sailors say they are an omen of bad weather
And call them the Children of Storm.

They gather in charcoal twilight
On a Skellig winter night,

Flashing question-marks of silver
On the underside

Of pared-nail, black-sickle wings,
Then take off for the Cape.

Thirteen thousand miles, round trip
From a *mille feuille* granite ledge

Over creamy North Atlantic thunderheads
To Africa's scorpion cliffs

Of lemon cloisonné, rose quartz, sand schist.
Hard to believe the same five grammes

Of feathers can zoom in like that
Without a compass, so precise,

From Africa back to where it hatched:
Black-igloo churches built of the rock they stand on

Recorded in the Annals of Innisfallen,
The Martyrology of Tallaght,

And gritty landmarks men have dubbed
Christ's Saddle and Monk's Grave.

In spring
The Priest's Stone watches for them like a lover

Praying, 'If there's one
Life to be saved

'Let it, however selfish, be
The one that's coming back to me.'

Like the poster of the French Lieutenant's Woman
Leaning in silhouette

At sunset
Against a shine-and-shadowboxing sea.

★

They're faithful to their rock. No *Casablanca*
For a storm petrel. No scalpel in the soul

When you hear 'As Time Goes By'
('I thought I told you never to play that song'),

Then walking off soft-focus in the mist
At night,

Having made your lover fly
To the other life

Where she, or he, belongs.
To miss you, as you'll miss

Her, or him, for ever.
Storm petrels wouldn't give a fucking feather

For sacrifice or grace of heart.
They'd see renunciation

As a stupid black-pearl egg
I've laid on the altar of your fatherhood.

I gave it to you easy. One-way flight.
The journey I'll make sure you don't come back from.

This is the long midnight
Of all our years together.

St Lucy's Day,
If we're talking the believing

Your mother raised you in,
The faith under your soul's skin.

The day I made a promise in my mind
That you and your kids

Would live in the same house OK
If not forever

Then for me, for now.
I had to darken out. A flare in wind

Like candles round the lawn
At our summer party.

When everyone else had gone, we lay
Looking up (well, I was) at a cloud of stars,

Surrounded by a ring of jewel-fires
From the Hardware Centre's *Plain Glass*

Votive Holders. When we woke in chill grey dawn
The tiny flames were out.

When you'd gone too, only my push-up bra
Was left on the flattened grass.

★

But back to storm petrels. It helps,
To keep your mind on outside things.

I'd like, in these last words, to tell
You how they lay

Their one and only egg in a chink of wall
Which they enter and leave at night.

They never sing, as we did all the time,
But recognize their mate

In the dark by a cry.
Her cry, and his.

For this is valediction.
From now on, you and I

Who once knew by telepathy
Across the crawly city

What each of us was feeling,
Will register each other only by

Unbidden radar. Odd, hypnopompic visions; rude
Dreams, lost in separate darknesses.

And in time, you,
For whom 'No love worked out somehow'

Except with me, who were never faithful to
Any woman longer than six months

Except these five years with me,
Will go back to philandering. You're on your own

And I can't help. I'm checking out
On a different flightpath now.

But somewhere in another galaxy,
Some parallel universe,

We'll still be what we were.
St Peter's birds,

Doing the impossible, walking on sea,
The outriders of storm.

Off-course maybe; blown,
Fragile; but together. Drawn

To their one and only mate
By magnetism, a cry

You recognize in the dark above all others,
And by faith.